A Guide to SEO Executive Skills

C. P. Kumar
Reiki Healer & Author
Roorkee - 247667, India

Disclaimer

While every effort has been made to ensure the accuracy and completeness of the content in this book, the author cannot guarantee that the information contained herein is error-free, up-to-date, or suitable for every individual circumstance.

The author shall not be held liable or responsible for any errors or omissions in the content of the book, nor for any damages, or losses that may arise from any actions taken based upon the suggestions or contents presented in the book.

Readers are advised to use their own judgment and discretion in applying the information provided in this book, and to consult with qualified professionals before taking any action based on the contents of this book. The author disclaims any and all liability or responsibility for any actions taken or not taken based on the information contained in this book.

DEDICATION

To every aspiring SEO executive, whose passion for unlocking the mysteries of the digital realm propels them forward. This book is dedicated to those who tirelessly navigate the ever-evolving landscape of search engine optimization, armed with a hunger for knowledge and an unwavering commitment to mastering the art and science of SEO.

In the spirit of exploration, this guide is dedicated to the curious minds diving into the intricacies of search engines, algorithms, and the dynamic field of online marketing. May your journey through these chapters be as enlightening as it is rewarding, propelling you to new heights in your SEO endeavors.

To the web architects and wordsmiths, the coding maestros and content creators, this dedication extends to those who understand the delicate balance between technical prowess and creative expression. Your dedication shapes the virtual landscapes we traverse, leaving an indelible mark on the digital tapestry.

To the ethical guardians of the digital realm, this book is dedicated to those who champion white hat tactics, steering clear of the shadows in their pursuit of optimization excellence. May your commitment to integrity and adherence to search engine guidelines shine as a beacon for others in the SEO community.

As we delve into the depths of SEO, this dedication is extended to the analysts, strategists, and trackers of performance metrics. Your keen insights and relentless pursuit of improvement inspire us all to push boundaries and exceed expectations.

Finally, to those with aspirations of advancing their SEO careers and shaping the future of the industry, this dedication echoes the collective ambition to stay ahead of trends, foster innovation, and embrace the opportunities for growth that SEO presents.

May this guide be a companion in your journey, offering insights, strategies, and inspiration to fuel your quest for SEO excellence.

C. P. Kumar

CONTENTS

PREFACE

In the vast expanse of the digital realm, where every keystroke and click echoes in the virtual corridors, search engine optimization (SEO) stands as the beacon guiding businesses and individuals through the labyrinth of the online landscape. This guide, "A Guide to SEO Executive Skills", is more than just a compilation of chapters; it is a roadmap designed to equip you with the skills and insights necessary to navigate the ever-evolving world of SEO.

In these pages, we embark on a journey that begins with the foundational principles of SEO. We delve into the very essence of this digital alchemy, defining SEO and unraveling its significance in a world where visibility and relevance are paramount. The role of an SEO Executive is explored, providing a comprehensive overview that sets the stage for the myriad skills and experiences awaiting exploration.

As we progress, we lift the veil on the enigmatic workings of search engines and algorithms. From the intricate dance of algorithms to the dynamic landscape of updates, we equip you with the knowledge needed to understand the heartbeat of the digital ecosystem. This guide goes beyond theory, delving into the practical requirements and industry nuances that shape the role of an SEO professional. Whether your journey leads you into the realms of online marketing, e-commerce, or web development, the insights garnered here will serve as your compass.

Website analysis and audit become second nature as we guide you through the process of dissecting digital landscapes. With a discerning eye, we identify areas for improvement, deletion, or revision, laying the groundwork for effective SEO strategies. The quest for powerful keywords becomes an art form, and the development of effective keyword strategies emerges as a cornerstone in your SEO repertoire.

From the intricacies of on-page SEO optimization to the nuances of off-page strategies, this guide covers the spectrum of skills demanded by the SEO executive. Technical prowess takes center stage, with chapters devoted to basic programming, web design skills, and the effective use of header tags. We demystify the realm of pay-per-click campaigns, offering insights into running successful campaigns and fine-tuning strategies based on performance metrics.

As we journey through the chapters, ethical considerations become our guiding principle. We explore the delicate balance between white hat and black hat tactics, urging practitioners to embrace ethical SEO practices and avoid violations of search engine guidelines. The symbiotic relationship between website navigation, design, and search engine ranking is unveiled, highlighting the collaborative efforts required for optimal performance.

Analytics and reporting tools become our trusted companions in the quest for SEO excellence. From Google Analytics to popular keyword tools, we equip you with the tools necessary to decipher the digital metrics that shape your online presence. Performance tracking becomes an art, with strategies to improve and track site performance, culminating in the compilation and presentation of comprehensive SEO performance reports.

Finally, we ascend to the pinnacle of SEO mastery. The chapters on advanced SEO strategies and career advancement are not just the culmination of knowledge but a call to action. As you explore advanced strategies and stay ahead of industry trends, this guide beckons you to develop the necessary skills for your role and explore the vast opportunities for career growth in the ever-expanding field of SEO.

This guide is more than a compendium of information; it is an invitation to immerse yourself in the dynamic world of SEO, to embrace the challenges and opportunities it presents, and to emerge not just as an executive but as a maestro orchestrating the symphony of digital success. Welcome to "A Guide to SEO Executive Skills". Your journey begins now.

C. P. Kumar
Reiki Healer
Former Scientist 'G', National Institute of Hydrology
Roorkee - 247667, India
Web: https://www.angelfire.com/nh/cpkumar/virgo.html

In the vast and ever-expanding digital universe, where information flows ceaselessly and online visibility is paramount, Search Engine Optimization (SEO) emerges as the guiding light for individuals and businesses alike. As we embark on this exploration, the chapters within "*A Guide to SEO Executive Skills*" aim to unravel the intricacies of SEO, starting with a comprehensive introduction to its fundamental principles.

Defining SEO

At its core, SEO is the art and science of optimizing online content to improve its visibility on search engine results pages. In a world where billions of searches are conducted daily, mastering the principles of SEO becomes a strategic imperative. It involves a holistic approach, encompassing various techniques and strategies to enhance a website's ranking on search engines like Google, Bing, and Yahoo.

SEO is not merely a technical endeavor; it's a dynamic process that blends creativity, analytics, and adaptability. It revolves around understanding the algorithms that govern search engines and tailoring content to align with these algorithms, ensuring that the most relevant and valuable information reaches the audience.

Importance of SEO

Why does SEO matter? The answer lies in the digital heartbeat of the modern era - search engines. The majority of online experiences begin with a search, making search engines the gateway to information, products, and services. A strong SEO strategy ensures that when individuals seek answers, solutions, or products related to a particular niche, your online presence is not only visible but prominently positioned.

SEO is the linchpin connecting businesses with their target audience. It transcends the realms of mere visibility; it's about fostering a meaningful online presence that resonates with the needs and preferences of the intended audience. A well-executed SEO strategy not only boosts rankings but also enhances user experience, credibility, and trust.

Overview of the Role of an SEO Executive

The success of an SEO strategy hinges on the expertise and acumen of SEO executives. These digital architects play a pivotal role in shaping the online narrative of a business or individual. Their responsibilities extend far beyond keyword optimization; they are custodians of online reputation, brand visibility, and digital success.

An SEO executive is not just a technician but a strategist, constantly adapting to the evolving algorithms of search engines. From understanding the nuances of content creation to deciphering analytics and implementing effective off-page strategies, the SEO executive is a multifaceted professional at the forefront of the digital battleground.

SEO executives are the bridge between the digital realm and business goals. They translate the language of algorithms into impactful strategies that elevate a brand's online presence. In the chapters to follow, we will delve into the intricacies of their role, exploring the skills, experiences, and insights necessary to excel in the dynamic field of SEO.

Conclusion: Setting the Stage for SEO Mastery

As we conclude this introductory exploration into the world of SEO, it becomes evident that SEO is not a mere technicality; it's a strategic imperative for anyone seeking relevance and visibility in the digital space. In the chapters that follow in "*A Guide to SEO Executive Skills*", we will embark on a journey through the foundational principles of SEO, understanding the algorithms that govern search engines, and unraveling the industry nuances that shape the role of an SEO executive.

This guide is not just a compilation of techniques; it's a roadmap to mastering the art and science of SEO. It's an invitation to explore the dynamic landscape of search engines, algorithms, and digital strategies. Whether you are a budding SEO professional or a seasoned executive looking to enhance your skills, this guide aims to be your trusted companion in the quest for SEO excellence. Welcome to the world of SEO, where visibility transforms into digital success, and the journey is as enriching as the destination.

Chapter 2. Understanding Search Engines and Algorithms

Introduction

In the vast landscape of the internet, where billions of web pages contend for attention, search engines emerge as the digital gatekeepers, guiding users to relevant information. As we delve into the chapters of "*A Guide to SEO Executive Skills*", understanding the inner workings of search engines and the algorithms that power them becomes crucial for anyone aspiring to navigate the dynamic field of SEO.

Search engines are the virtual compass guiding users through the vast expanse of the internet. Google, Bing, Yahoo, and other search engines serve as the conduits between users and the wealth of information available online. In this digital age, where information is currency, mastering the intricacies of search engines is paramount for individuals and businesses alike.

Explanation of How Search Engines Work

At its core, a search engine is a sophisticated information retrieval system designed to deliver the most relevant and valuable content in response to a user's query. The journey begins with the deployment of web crawlers or spiders - automated programs that traverse the internet, scouring web pages, and indexing their content.

Once a user enters a search query, the search engine's algorithm swings into action. The algorithm sifts through the vast index of web pages, considering various factors to determine the relevance and significance of each page to the user's query. These factors range from keyword relevance and content quality to the authority and credibility of the website.

Search engines are not static; they continuously evolve to enhance user experience and provide more accurate results. This evolution is driven by updates to search engine algorithms, shaping the way content is ranked and displayed.

Overview of Search Engine Algorithms and Updates

Search engine algorithms are complex mathematical formulas that assess and rank web pages based on numerous criteria. While the exact algorithms used by search engines are closely guarded secrets, certain principles guide SEO professionals in optimizing content for better visibility.

One of the most well-known algorithms is Google's PageRank, which evaluates the importance of web pages based on the quantity and quality of links pointing to them. However, modern algorithms take a multifaceted approach, considering factors such as user experience, relevance, and mobile-friendliness.

Search engines regularly update their algorithms to stay ahead of evolving user behaviors and technological advancements. These updates, such as Google's Panda, Penguin, and Hummingbird updates, have significant implications for SEO strategies. Panda targets low-quality content, Penguin penalizes manipulative link-building practices, and Hummingbird focuses on understanding user intent, emphasizing conversational queries.

Keeping abreast of these updates is imperative for SEO executives. It ensures that optimization strategies align with the current preferences and priorities of search engines, maintaining or improving a website's ranking in search results.

Conclusion

Understanding search engines and their algorithms is akin to navigating a constantly changing digital sea. SEO executives must be adept sailors, attuned to the winds of algorithmic updates and the undercurrents of user behavior. As we progress through the chapters of "*A Guide to SEO Executive Skills*", the insights gained here will serve as the foundation for crafting effective strategies that resonate with the algorithms governing the digital landscape.

This understanding is not merely a technicality but a strategic advantage in the competitive realm of online visibility. It empowers SEO professionals to optimize content not just for search engines but for the individuals seeking valuable information. Welcome to the realm where algorithms and user intent converge, shaping the destiny of digital content.

Introduction

In the dynamic field of Search Engine Optimization (SEO), success is not just about understanding algorithms but also about possessing a diverse set of skills and experiences. As we embark on the chapters of "*A Guide to SEO Executive Skills*", we delve into the prerequisites and industry nuances that shape the role of an SEO professional.

The landscape of SEO is not static; it's a dynamic ecosystem that demands adaptability and a nuanced understanding of digital marketing trends. The chapters that follow provide a roadmap for aspiring SEO executives, guiding them through the essential requirements and offering insights into the industry contexts that define their roles.

Experience and Skills Required for SEO

SEO is more than just optimizing web content for search engines; it requires a multifaceted skill set and a wealth of experiences. At its core, an effective SEO professional is a strategic thinker, an analytical mind, and a creative problem solver.

1. Analytical Skills

An SEO executive needs to decipher complex analytics and draw actionable insights. Analytical skills are crucial for understanding user behavior, tracking performance metrics, and refining strategies based on data-driven decisions.

2. Technical Proficiency

While not every SEO professional needs to be a programmer, a basic understanding of HTML, CSS, and web development is advantageous. Technical proficiency ensures effective communication with web developers and a comprehensive understanding of technical SEO aspects.

3. Content Creation and Marketing

SEO is inherently tied to content. The ability to create original and compelling content, aligned with SEO strategies, is a key skill. From crafting engaging headlines to developing effective calls-to-action, content creation is an art that SEO professionals must master.

4. Adaptability

In the rapidly evolving digital landscape, adaptability is non-negotiable. SEO executives must stay abreast of algorithmic updates, industry trends, and emerging technologies to ensure their strategies remain effective.

5. Communication Skills

Effective communication is paramount in the collaborative world of SEO. SEO executives must articulate their strategies, insights, and recommendations to diverse stakeholders, from clients to developers.

Industry Context

Understanding the specific requirements of different industries is integral to tailoring SEO strategies for maximum impact. The contexts of online marketing, e-commerce, and web development shape the expectations and goals of SEO professionals in distinctive ways.

1. Online Marketing

In the realm of online marketing, SEO is a linchpin. It complements other digital marketing strategies, such as social media marketing and email campaigns, to create a comprehensive online presence. SEO executives in this context must align their strategies with broader marketing goals and collaborate seamlessly with marketing teams.

2. E-commerce

For e-commerce businesses, SEO is the gateway to visibility and sales. The ability to optimize product pages, enhance user experience, and navigate the complexities of e-commerce platforms is crucial. SEO executives must understand the intricacies of product listings, user reviews, and the unique challenges posed by online shopping.

3. Web Development

Collaboration with web developers is intrinsic to successful SEO. In the context of web development, SEO executives need a nuanced understanding of website structures, coding practices, and user experience design. Consulting with web developers ensures that SEO strategies seamlessly integrate with the technical aspects of website development.

Conclusion

As we conclude this exploration into the requirements and industry overview of SEO, it becomes evident that SEO is not a one-size-fits-all profession. It's a dynamic field that demands continual learning and adaptation. The SEO executive is not just an optimizer of keywords; they are architects of digital success, weaving together technical proficiency, analytical acumen, and creative flair.

In the chapters that follow, we delve deeper into the intricacies of website analysis, keyword research, on-page and off-page optimization, and advanced SEO strategies. Armed with the foundational knowledge gained here, SEO professionals can navigate the complex terrain of the digital landscape, ensuring their skills remain sharp and their strategies remain effective in the ever-evolving world of SEO.

Introduction

In the intricate dance of digital optimization, the cornerstone of any successful SEO strategy lies in a thorough website analysis and audit. As we delve into the chapters of *"A Guide to SEO Executive Skills"*, this exploration becomes the compass guiding SEO executives through the nuanced process of dissecting, evaluating, and optimizing websites for optimal performance.

Before delving into the intricacies of website analysis, it's crucial to recognize the pivotal role it plays in the overall SEO landscape. A website serves as the digital storefront for businesses and individuals alike, and optimizing its structure and content is fundamental to achieving visibility on search engine results pages.

Website analysis and audit are not mere technical exercises; they are strategic imperatives. In the following sections, we will unravel the key components of a comprehensive website analysis, exploring how SEO executives can navigate this process to enhance a website's efficacy and impact.

Conducting a Comprehensive Website Analysis

Website analysis involves a meticulous examination of various elements that contribute to a website's performance, visibility, and user experience. It's a systematic process that enables SEO executives to identify strengths, weaknesses, and areas ripe for improvement. Let's delve into the key aspects of conducting a comprehensive website analysis.

1. User Experience (UX)

The user experience is a critical factor in determining a website's effectiveness. SEO executives must assess the overall design, navigation, and accessibility of a website to ensure it meets user expectations. Factors such as page load speed, mobile responsiveness, and intuitive navigation significantly impact user experience.

2. Content Quality and Relevance

Content is the lifeblood of a website. A thorough analysis involves evaluating the quality, relevance, and uniqueness of the content. SEO executives must ensure that the content aligns with the website's objectives, speaks to the target audience, and adheres to SEO best practices.

3. Technical SEO Factors

Technical SEO elements, including website architecture, URL structure, and metadata, play a crucial role in search engine rankings. SEO executives need to assess these factors to identify areas where technical improvements can be made for better visibility.

4. Backlink Profile

Backlinks are a vote of confidence from other websites. A website's backlink profile influences its authority in the eyes of search engines. Analyzing the quality and diversity of backlinks helps SEO professionals understand the website's standing within the digital ecosystem.

5. Keyword Optimization

Effective use of keywords is fundamental to SEO. SEO executives must scrutinize the website's use of keywords in titles, headers, and body content. Keyword analysis provides insights into the website's relevance to specific search queries.

Identifying Areas for Improvement, Deletion, or Revision

Once the website analysis is complete, the next step is to translate insights into action. This involves identifying specific areas that require improvement, deletion, or revision to enhance the website's overall performance. The optimization process is an art that involves balancing technical precision with creative finesse.

1. Optimizing Content

Based on the analysis, SEO executives may identify content that needs improvement or revision. This could involve rewriting copy for clarity, relevance, or SEO optimization. Outdated or redundant content may be flagged for deletion.

2. Technical Enhancements

Addressing technical SEO issues is paramount for optimal performance. SEO executives may recommend improvements to website architecture, URL structures, and metadata. Resolving issues related to page load speed and mobile responsiveness contributes to a positive user experience.

3. Backlink Cleanup

A robust backlink profile is built on quality, not quantity. SEO executives may engage in a backlink cleanup process, identifying and disavowing low-quality or spammy backlinks. This ensures a healthier and more authoritative backlink profile.

4. Keyword Refinement

Based on keyword analysis, SEO executives may refine the use of keywords across the website. This could involve strategically incorporating high-value keywords into content, headers, and metadata to enhance relevance and visibility.

Conclusion

In the intricate tapestry of SEO, website analysis and audit serve as the loom upon which success is woven. The insights gained from a comprehensive analysis guide SEO executives in transforming a website from a mere digital entity to a dynamic and impactful online presence.

As we conclude this exploration into website analysis and audit, it's crucial to recognize that the journey doesn't end here. The digital landscape is ever-evolving, and SEO excellence requires continual assessment and adaptation. In the subsequent chapters of *"A Guide to SEO Executive Skills"*, we will unravel the intricacies of keyword research, on-page and off-page optimization, technical SEO skills, and more.

Armed with the knowledge gained from website analysis, SEO executives are poised to embark on a journey of optimization and enhancement. Welcome to the realm where analysis transforms into action, and websites become not just pages on the internet but strategic assets in the digital marketplace.

Introduction

In the intricate realm of Search Engine Optimization (SEO), where visibility is paramount, the foundation of success rests upon the meticulous craft of keyword research and strategy. As we embark on the chapters of "*A Guide to SEO Executive Skills*", the exploration into choosing powerful keywords and developing effective strategies unfolds as a crucial chapter in the SEO narrative.

In the vast orchestra of the internet, where every click represents a note, keywords emerge as the lyrical threads weaving through the digital symphony. They are the linguistic keys that unlock the doors to online visibility, ensuring that the right audience finds and resonates with the digital content. This exploration into keyword research and strategy is not merely a technical exercise but a profound journey into the essence of digital significance.

Choosing Powerful and Profitable Keywords

At its core, keyword research is a quest to understand the language of search engines and the intentions of users. It is a delicate balance between choosing words that align with the content of a website and selecting terms that users are likely to input into search queries. This nuanced dance involves several key considerations.

1. Relevance to Content

The first criterion in choosing keywords is relevance. Keywords should accurately reflect the themes and topics addressed on a website. They serve as digital signposts, guiding both users and search engines to the heart of the content.

2. Search Volume and Competition

The effectiveness of keywords lies not just in their relevance but also in their search volume and competition. High search volume indicates significant user interest, but it also intensifies competition. SEO executives must strike a balance, selecting keywords that are both popular and strategically viable.

3. Long-Tail Keywords

Long-tail keywords, comprising more extended and specific phrases, play a pivotal role in targeting niche audiences. While they may have lower search volumes individually, they collectively contribute to a website's visibility and attract users with specific intents.

4. User Intent

Understanding user intent is fundamental to effective keyword selection. Keywords should align with the varied intents of users, whether informational, transactional, or navigational. This ensures that the content meets the expectations of those entering specific search queries.

Developing Effective Keyword Strategies

Choosing keywords is the overture, and developing effective strategies is the orchestration that brings the digital symphony to life. Keyword strategies go beyond mere inclusion in content; they involve a thoughtful approach to placement, optimization, and adaptation. Let's delve into the components of crafting effective keyword strategies.

1. Strategic Placement in Content

Once keywords are selected, their strategic placement within content becomes pivotal. SEO executives must integrate keywords seamlessly into titles, headers, and body content, ensuring a natural flow that resonates with both users and search engines.

2. Optimizing Metadata

Metadata, including title tags and meta descriptions, serves as the digital introduction to a website. Keywords in metadata contribute to search engine visibility and influence click-through rates. Strategic optimization of metadata enhances a website's presence in search engine results pages (SERPs).

3. Creating Topic Clusters

An advanced keyword strategy involves creating topic clusters - groups of interlinked content centered around a core topic. This not only enhances the thematic relevance of a website but also strengthens its overall authority in the eyes of search engines.

4. Adapting to Algorithmic Changes

Search engine algorithms are dynamic, and keyword strategies must adapt accordingly. Regular monitoring of algorithmic updates ensures that keyword strategies remain effective and aligned with the evolving preferences of search engines.

Conclusion

As we conclude this exploration into keyword research and strategy, it becomes evident that keywords are more than strings of characters; they are the conduits through which digital impact is achieved. The meticulous selection of powerful and profitable keywords, coupled with thoughtful strategies, transforms a website from a digital whisper to a resonant voice in the vast digital expanse.

In the subsequent chapters of *"A Guide to SEO Executive Skills"*, we will delve deeper into the intricacies of on-page and off-page optimization, technical SEO skills, and the multifaceted aspects of content creation and marketing. Armed with the foundational knowledge gained here, SEO executives are poised to orchestrate their websites' visibility and significance in the ever-evolving symphony of the digital realm.

Welcome to the journey where words transcend into impact, and digital presence becomes a melody that echoes across the vast corridors of the internet.

Introduction

In the intricate tapestry of Search Engine Optimization (SEO), on-page optimization stands as the artisanal craft of sculpting digital excellence. As we immerse ourselves in the chapters of "*A Guide to SEO Executive Skills*", the exploration into on-page SEO optimization unfolds as a pivotal chapter, delving into the art and science of refining website elements for maximum visibility and impact.

On-page SEO optimization is not merely a technical endeavor; it is the conscious art of curating the elements that users interact with directly. From the compelling headlines that capture attention to the body copy that engages and the overall website content that informs and resonates, on-page optimization transforms a website into a dynamic and user-centric entity.

Writing Effective Headlines, Body Copy, and Website Content

1. Captivating Headlines

The journey into on-page SEO optimization begins with crafting headlines that not only capture attention but also encapsulate the essence of the content. Headlines serve as the initial touchpoint for users and search engines alike. They should be concise, compelling, and rich in relevant keywords, acting as a beacon that draws users deeper into the digital narrative.

2. Engaging Body Copy

Beyond the allure of headlines lies the body copy - the substance that keeps users immersed. On-page optimization involves writing body copy that is not only informative but also engaging. The content should be structured for readability, incorporating headers, subheadings, and bullet points to enhance user experience. SEO executives become digital storytellers, weaving narratives that cater to both human readers and search engine algorithms.

3. Informative Website Content

The overarching goal of on-page optimization is to create a digital space that is not just discoverable but also valuable. Website content should provide information that meets user intent, answering queries and fulfilling the expectations set by search queries. Whether it's blog posts, product descriptions, or informative articles, on-page SEO ensures that the content is aligned with user needs and preferences.

Optimizing Websites with Optimal Keywords

In the symphony of on-page optimization, keywords take center stage. Optimal integration of keywords into headlines, body copy, and overall content is essential for aligning a website's thematic relevance with search engine algorithms. This involves a strategic approach that balances the natural flow of content with the intentional inclusion of keywords.

1. Strategic Keyword Placement

On-page SEO optimization requires a nuanced understanding of where and how to place keywords for maximum impact. Headlines, especially the H1 tag, should incorporate primary keywords to signal their importance to search engines. Subheadings and body copy should seamlessly integrate variations of keywords, enhancing thematic relevance.

2. Avoiding Keyword Stuffing

While keywords are the pillars of on-page optimization, excessive use can lead to keyword stuffing - a practice frowned upon by search engines. SEO executives must strike a balance, ensuring that keywords contribute to the overall narrative without compromising the natural flow of language. This not only enhances user experience but also maintains credibility in the eyes of search engines.

3. Long-Tail Keywords for Precision

On-page optimization extends beyond conventional keywords to include long-tail keywords - specific phrases that cater to niche queries. Integrating long-tail keywords into content enhances the website's visibility for users with distinct intents, contributing to a comprehensive on-page SEO strategy.

Conclusion

As we conclude this exploration into on-page SEO optimization, it becomes evident that this practice is not a mechanical checklist but a symphony of digital excellence. The effective interplay between headlines, body copy, and website content, strategically woven with optimal keywords, transforms a website into a dynamic and resonant entity in the digital landscape.

In the subsequent chapters of "*A Guide to SEO Executive Skills*", we will unravel the intricacies of off-page SEO strategies, delve into the technical skills required for SEO excellence, and explore advanced strategies for digital prominence. Armed with the foundational knowledge gained here, SEO executives are poised to orchestrate their websites' visibility and impact in the ever-evolving digital symphony.

Welcome to the realm where on-page optimization transcends the technical and becomes an art form - a symphony of digital elements that harmonize to create an impactful and memorable online presence.

Introduction

In the expansive realm of Search Engine Optimization (SEO), the exploration of off-page strategies stands as the compass guiding SEO executives through the vast digital landscape. Off-page SEO refers to optimization efforts that take place outside of your own website and involve factors that influence your site's visibility in search engine results. As we delve into the chapters of "*A Guide to SEO Executive Skills*", the intricacies of off-page SEO strategies unfold - a multifaceted journey encompassing content strategies and the strategic use of coding to enhance digital prominence.

While on-page optimization shapes the content users directly interact with, off-page SEO strategies extend beyond the boundaries of a website. They involve activities that take place away from the site but impact its visibility and authority. Off-page SEO is the collaborative dance between a website and the broader digital ecosystem, where content strategies and coding intricacies play pivotal roles.

Implementing Off-Page SEO Content Strategies

1. Link Building

At the heart of off-page SEO content strategies lies the art of link building. Links are digital endorsements, signaling to search engines that a website is authoritative and relevant. SEO executives engage in the strategic cultivation of backlinks - links from external sites pointing to their own. These could be earned through compelling content, outreach efforts, or collaborations within the industry.

2. Social Media Presence

The digital footprint of a website extends to social media platforms. Off-page SEO involves leveraging social media channels to amplify content reach, foster engagement, and build a community around the brand. Social signals, such as likes, shares, and comments, contribute to a website's perceived authority.

3. Content Collaboration and Outreach

SEO executives actively seek opportunities for content collaboration and outreach within their industry. Guest blogging, co-authored articles, and participation in industry forums foster a sense of community and position the website as an authoritative voice in its niche.

Utilizing Coding for Improved SEO

1. Schema Markup

Schema markup, also known as structured data, is a code added to a website's HTML to provide search engines with more detailed information about the content on the page. It helps search engines better understand the context and meaning of the information, which can enhance the way search results are displayed. Schema markup uses a standardized vocabulary to tag and categorize content, making it more accessible to search engine algorithms.

Coding comes to the forefront in off-page SEO through the strategic use of schema markup. This structured data format provides search engines with additional context about the content on a website. Implementing schema markup enhances the likelihood of rich snippets appearing in search results, providing more information to users and improving click-through rates.

2. Canonical Tags

Canonical tags are HTML elements used to address duplicate content issues on a website. They help search engines understand the preferred or canonical version of a particular page when there are multiple versions with similar or identical content. The canonical tag is placed in the head section of the HTML code and points to the preferred URL.

SEO executives utilize canonical tags within the website's HTML to signal the preferred version of a page when multiple versions exist. This helps prevent duplicate content issues, ensuring that search engines attribute authority to the correct page.

3. Open Graph Protocol

The Open Graph Protocol (OGP) is a set of metadata tags that website developers can include in the HTML of their pages to control the way content appears when shared on social media platforms. Developed by Facebook, the Open Graph Protocol helps standardize the representation of shared content, ensuring a consistent and appealing display across various social media networks.

In the realm of social media, the Open Graph Protocol allows websites to control how their content appears when shared on platforms like Facebook. SEO executives employ coding techniques to optimize how content is presented, enhancing its visual appeal and click-through potential.

Conclusion

As we conclude this exploration into off-page SEO strategies, it becomes evident that this realm is a dynamic interplay of content collaboration and technical finesse. Off-page SEO is the symphony where a website harmonizes with the broader digital chorus, leveraging content strategies and coding intricacies for optimal visibility and authority.

In the subsequent chapters of "*A Guide to SEO Executive Skills*", we will unravel the technical SEO skills required for excellence, explore the nuances of pay-per-click (PPC) campaigns, and delve into the art of content creation and marketing. Armed with the knowledge gained here, SEO executives are poised to navigate the digital landscape and orchestrate their websites' prominence in the ever-evolving symphony of online presence.

Welcome to the realm where off-page strategies transcend the technical and become a collaborative dance - a symphony of digital elements that harmonize to create an impactful and memorable online presence.

Introduction

In the intricate landscape of Search Engine Optimization (SEO), technical prowess forms the bedrock upon which digital excellence is built. As we navigate the chapters of *"A Guide to SEO Executive Skills"*, the exploration into technical SEO skills unfolds - a journey encompassing basic programming, web design acumen, and the strategic utilization of header tags.

Technical SEO skills are the unseen engine propelling a website's visibility and efficacy in the digital realm. While content captures attention, technical optimization ensures that the website is not only discoverable by search engines but also aligned with their algorithms. This chapter delves into the essential technical skills that empower SEO executives to navigate the intricacies of the digital landscape.

Basic Programming and Web Design Skills for SEO

1. HTML and CSS Proficiency

At the core of technical SEO lies a fundamental proficiency in HTML and CSS. HTML (Hypertext Markup Language) is the standard markup language for creating and structuring web pages. It uses tags to define elements such as headings, paragraphs, links, images, and other content, enabling browsers to interpret and display information on the internet. CSS (Cascading Style Sheets) is a stylesheet language used to describe the presentation and formatting of HTML or XML documents, defining how elements should be displayed on web pages.

SEO executives with basic programming skills can navigate the code underlying web pages, making strategic adjustments to enhance search engine visibility. Understanding the structure of HTML tags and the styling capabilities of CSS allows for precise modifications that align with SEO objectives.

2. JavaScript Understanding

JavaScript is a high-level, interpreted programming language primarily used for enhancing interactivity and dynamic behavior on websites. It allows developers to manipulate webpage content, respond to user actions, and create dynamic, client-side functionality.

As websites become more dynamic, an understanding of JavaScript becomes increasingly valuable. SEO executives equipped with JavaScript knowledge can assess its impact on search engine crawling and indexing. Additionally, they can collaborate effectively with web developers to ensure that JavaScript elements do not hinder search engine accessibility.

3. Website Speed Optimization

Website speed, also known as page speed or site speed, refers to the time it takes for a web page to load completely in a user's browser. It is a crucial aspect of the user experience and can impact a website's performance, search engine rankings, and overall user satisfaction.

Technical SEO extends to the optimization of website speed, a crucial factor in both user experience and search engine rankings. Basic programming skills enable SEO professionals to identify and address issues that may impede loading times, such as large image files, unnecessary scripts, or inefficient coding structures.

Effective Use of Header Tags

1. Significance of Header Tags

Header tags (H1 to H6) play a pivotal role in structuring content and signaling its hierarchy to search engines. SEO executives with technical acumen understand the significance of these tags in creating a logical and well-organized content hierarchy. The H1 tag, in particular, carries substantial weight in conveying the primary topic of a page.

2. Optimizing Header Tags for Keywords

Effective use of header tags involves strategic optimization for keywords. SEO professionals integrate relevant keywords into headers, enhancing thematic relevance and signaling the content's topical focus to search engines. This not only contributes to on-page SEO but also aids in creating a user-friendly content structure.

3. Avoiding Header Tag Overuse

While header tags are instrumental in content organization, their excessive use can dilute their impact. SEO executives with technical proficiency strike a balance, employing header tags judiciously to maintain a clear structure without overwhelming the content with excessive formatting.

Conclusion

As we conclude this exploration into technical SEO skills, it becomes evident that technical proficiency is not a mere supplement to SEO strategy but an integral aspect of mastery. Basic programming skills, web design acumen, and a strategic approach to header tags form the tapestry of technical SEO excellence.

In the subsequent chapters of "*A Guide to SEO Executive Skills*", we will delve into the intricacies of pay-per-click (PPC) campaigns, explore the nuances of content creation and marketing, and uncover advanced SEO strategies for digital prominence. Armed with the foundational knowledge gained here, SEO executives are poised to orchestrate their websites' technical excellence in the ever-evolving symphony of online presence.

Welcome to the realm where technical SEO skills transcend the technical and become the language through which websites communicate their digital significance to both users and search engines.

Introduction

In the dynamic realm of digital marketing, Pay-Per-Click (PPC) campaigns emerge as the vanguard of strategic visibility. As we embark on the chapters of "*A Guide to SEO Executive Skills*", the exploration into PPC campaigns unfolds - a journey delving into the intricacies of running successful campaigns, the art of adjustments based on performance metrics, and the profound impact of PPC on digital prominence.

PPC, or Pay-Per-Click, campaigns are a form of online advertising where advertisers pay a fee each time their ad is clicked. These campaigns are commonly used to drive traffic to websites, generate leads, or increase sales.

PPC campaigns represent a symbiotic dance between advertisers and digital platforms, where every click carries the promise of engagement. Unlike organic methods, PPC allows advertisers to bid for ad placements, ensuring their content reaches a targeted audience. This chapter explores the multifaceted landscape of PPC, unraveling the nuances that empower SEO executives to harness its potential.

Running Successful PPC Campaigns

1. Keyword Research and Selection

The foundation of a successful PPC campaign lies in meticulous keyword research and selection. SEO executives delve into understanding user intent, identifying relevant keywords, and crafting compelling ad copies that align with searcher expectations. Strategic keyword targeting ensures that the ads resonate with the right audience.

2. Compelling Ad Copies

In the realm of PPC, every word carries weight. SEO executives leverage their content creation skills to craft ad copies that are not only concise but also compelling. Ad copies should convey value propositions, call-to-action statements, and unique selling points, enticing users to click and explore further.

3. Landing Page Optimization

The journey doesn't end with a click; it begins with a well-optimized landing page. SEO executives ensure that the landing page aligns seamlessly with the ad content, providing a cohesive user experience. Optimization involves clear messaging, relevant content, and strategically placed calls-to-action to guide users toward desired actions.

Adjusting PPC Campaigns Based on Performance

1. Monitoring Key Performance Indicators (KPIs)

Key Performance Indicators (KPIs) are measurable metrics that organizations use to evaluate their performance and progress toward specific goals. KPIs help assess the effectiveness of various business processes and strategies. The selection of KPIs depends on the objectives and priorities of a particular business or project.

The success of PPC campaigns hinges on the vigilant monitoring of key performance indicators. SEO executives track metrics such as click-through rates (CTR), conversion rates, and cost per click (CPC) to assess campaign effectiveness.

Click-Through Rate (CTR) is the percentage of users who click on a specific link or ad out of the total number of users who view it. Conversion rate is the percentage of website visitors who take a desired action, such as making a purchase or filling out a form. Cost Per Click (CPC) is the amount an advertiser pays for each click on their advertisement in a pay-per-click (PPC) marketing campaign.

These KPIs provide insights into user behavior and the overall impact of the campaign.

2. A/B Testing for Optimization

A/B testing, also known as split testing, is a method of comparing two versions (A and B) of a webpage, email, or other content to determine which performs better based on a predefined metric, such as click-through rates, conversion rates, or engagement metrics.

SEO executives embrace A/B testing as a strategic tool for optimization. This involves creating variations of ad elements, such as headlines, ad copies, or visuals, and testing them against each other to identify the most effective components. A/B testing allows for continuous refinement, ensuring that campaigns evolve based on real-time performance data.

3. Budget Allocation and Bid Management

Effective PPC management involves a judicious allocation of budget and strategic bid management. SEO executives analyze data to identify high-performing keywords and allocate budget accordingly. Bid management ensures that bids align with campaign goals and respond to market dynamics to maximize ROI.

Conclusion

As we conclude this exploration into PPC campaigns, it becomes evident that the landscape is not static; it's a dynamic symphony that requires constant tuning. Running successful campaigns and adjusting based on performance metrics is a continuous dance - a strategic choreography that adapts to the ever-shifting digital stage.

In the subsequent chapters of "*A Guide to SEO Executive Skills*", we will unravel the nuances of content creation and marketing, explore the ethical considerations of White Hat and Black Hat tactics, and delve into advanced SEO strategies for digital prominence. Armed with the foundational knowledge gained here, SEO executives are poised to navigate the digital advertising frontier and orchestrate impactful PPC campaigns in the ever-evolving symphony of online presence.

Welcome to the realm where PPC campaigns transcend the transactional and become an orchestrated cadence - a digital symphony that resonates with the audience and elevates the brand's visibility in the competitive digital landscape.

Introduction

In the expansive realm of online presence, content emerges as the lifeblood that fuels engagement, communicates value, and elevates a brand's digital significance. As we delve into the chapters of "*A Guide to SEO Executive Skills*", the exploration into content creation and marketing unfolds - a journey encompassing the craft of writing original and powerful SEO content, and the strategic deployment of effective call-to-action statements.

Content creation and marketing transcend mere communication; they represent the art and science of digital expression. In the dynamic landscape of SEO, content serves as the bridge between brands and audiences, and its creation and strategic dissemination are pivotal for building a robust online presence.

Writing Original and Powerful SEO Content

1. Understanding Audience Intent

At the core of content creation lies an understanding of audience intent. SEO executives embark on a journey to comprehend the needs, questions, and interests of their target audience. This empathetic approach ensures that the content not only aligns with search engine algorithms but also resonates with the real-time needs of users.

2. Keyword Integration for Relevance

SEO content is a delicate balance between creativity and strategic keyword integration. SEO executives infuse originality into their writing while strategically incorporating relevant keywords. This dual approach ensures that the content ranks well on search engines and provides valuable information to users.

3. Crafting Compelling Headlines and Introductions

The journey of content engagement begins with headlines and introductions. SEO executives master the art of crafting headlines that capture attention and introductions that provide a glimpse of the value within. These elements act as digital invitations, enticing users to delve deeper into the content.

Developing Effective Call-to-Action Statements

1. Strategic Placement and Clarity

A call-to-action (CTA) is a prompt or directive in a piece of content, typically designed to encourage the audience to take a specific action, such as clicking a button, signing up for a newsletter, making a purchase, or engaging in some other desired behavior.

Call-to-action (CTA) statements serve as the digital cues guiding users toward desired actions. SEO executives strategically place CTAs within content, ensuring they are clear, compelling, and aligned with the overarching goals of the website. Whether it's encouraging a purchase, sign-up, or further exploration, CTAs are woven seamlessly into the content fabric.

2. Variety in CTA Elements

The effectiveness of a CTA lies not just in its clarity but also in its variety. SEO executives experiment with different CTA elements, such as buttons, text links, or interactive prompts, to cater to diverse user preferences. A well-crafted CTA resonates with the user, eliciting a response that aligns with the website's objectives.

3. Aligning CTAs with User Journey

Effective content marketing involves understanding the user journey and strategically aligning CTAs with different stages. Whether a user is in the discovery phase or on the verge of conversion, SEO executives tailor CTAs to guide users seamlessly through their digital journey, ensuring a cohesive and impactful experience.

Conclusion

As we conclude this exploration into content creation and marketing, it becomes evident that this realm is not a monologue but a dynamic conversation. Writing original and powerful SEO content, coupled with the strategic deployment of effective call-to-action statements, transforms content from a mere presence to a catalyst for engagement and conversion.

In the subsequent chapters of *"A Guide to SEO Executive Skills"*, we will unravel the nuances of ethical SEO practices, explore the intricacies of website navigation and design, and delve into advanced SEO strategies for digital prominence. Armed with the foundational knowledge gained here, SEO executives are poised to orchestrate the harmonious intersection of content and conversion in the ever-evolving symphony of online presence.

Welcome to the realm where content creation and marketing transcend the transactional and become a harmonious digital symphony - a narrative that resonates

with audiences and elevates brands in the competitive
digital landscape.

Introduction

In the ever-evolving landscape of Search Engine Optimization (SEO), ethical considerations form the bedrock upon which digital prominence stands. As we explore the chapters of *"A Guide to SEO Executive Skills"*, the investigation into White Hat and Black Hat tactics unfolds - a journey encompassing the nuances of ethical SEO practices, the imperative of avoiding violations of search engine guidelines, and the profound impact these choices have on digital success.

White hat tactics refer to ethical and legitimate strategies used in various fields, including SEO, digital marketing, and cybersecurity, to achieve positive outcomes without violating rules or regulations. Black hat tactics involve unethical and often manipulative techniques aimed at achieving quick results or gaining an unfair advantage. These practices can lead to negative consequences, such as penalties from search engines, legal action, or damage to reputation.

SEO is not just a technical endeavor; it's a moral compass that guides digital practitioners through the ethical spectrum. White Hat and Black Hat tactics represent the dual pathways - one leading to sustainable success through ethical practices, and the other tempting with shortcuts that risk long-term consequences. This chapter delves into the ethical considerations that define SEO excellence.

Understanding Ethical SEO Practices

1. Content Quality and Relevance

At the heart of White Hat SEO lies a commitment to content quality and relevance. Ethical SEO practitioners prioritize creating valuable, informative, and engaging content that caters to user intent. This approach not only aligns with search engine algorithms but also establishes a website as a reliable source within its niche.

2. Natural Link Building

White Hat SEO practitioners understand that link building is not about quantity but quality. Ethical link building involves earning backlinks through valuable content, collaborations, and industry relationships. This organic approach to link acquisition not only builds authority but also mitigates the risk of penalties from search engines.

3. User-Centric Optimization

Ethical SEO practices place users at the center of optimization efforts. Websites are designed and optimized with user experience in mind, ensuring easy navigation, clear information presentation, and a seamless journey through the digital landscape. Prioritizing user satisfaction contributes to long-term success and positive user engagement metrics.

Avoiding Violations of Search Engine Guidelines

1. Keyword Stuffing

One of the hallmarks of Black Hat SEO is the practice of keyword stuffing - cramming content with excessive keywords in an attempt to manipulate search engine rankings. SEO executives avoiding ethical pitfalls understand that keyword usage should be natural, contributing to readability and relevance rather than compromising content quality.

2. Cloaking and Hidden Text

Black Hat tactics often involve cloaking, where the content presented to search engines differs from what users see. Hidden text, invisible to users but readable by search engines, is another deceptive practice. Ethical SEO practitioners refrain from such tactics, as they violate the transparency expected by both users and search engines.

3. Link Schemes and Manipulation

Black Hat SEO may resort to link schemes, purchasing links, or engaging in manipulative practices to artificially inflate a website's link profile. This not only risks penalties but also compromises the integrity of the digital ecosystem. Ethical SEO executives understand the importance of genuine link-building efforts.

Conclusion

As we conclude this exploration into White Hat and Black Hat tactics, it becomes evident that ethical considerations are not just a choice but a moral imperative. The decisions made in the realm of SEO have profound consequences on a website's long-term success and its relationship with users and search engines.

In the subsequent chapters of "*A Guide to SEO Executive Skills*", we will delve into the intricacies of website navigation and design, explore analytics and reporting tools for informed decision-making, and uncover advanced SEO strategies for digital prominence. Armed with the foundational knowledge gained here, SEO executives are poised to navigate the ethical spectrum and orchestrate digital success in the ever-evolving symphony of online presence.

Welcome to the realm where ethical SEO practices transcend the transactional and become the moral compass guiding websites toward sustained success - a digital symphony that resonates with integrity, reliability, and long-term relevance.

Introduction

In the dynamic arena of online presence, the architecture of a website stands as the silent orchestrator of user experience and search engine visibility. As we navigate the chapters of *"A Guide to SEO Executive Skills"*, the exploration into website navigation and design unfolds - a journey delving into the collaborative process of consulting with web designers for improved navigation and the strategic artistry of enhancing search engine ranking through design.

Website navigation and design are not mere aesthetic choices; they are the fundamental building blocks that shape the digital journey for users and signal relevance to search engines. This chapter embarks on the exploration of how the thoughtful interplay of design and navigation contributes to a harmonious user experience and elevates a website's prominence in the digital landscape.

Consulting with Web Designers for Improved Navigation

1. Understanding User Behavior

Effective website navigation begins with a profound understanding of user behavior. SEO executives collaborate with web designers to analyze user journeys, identify common pathways, and anticipate user needs. This collaborative approach ensures that navigation is intuitive, minimizing user friction and enhancing overall satisfaction.

2. Streamlining Information Architecture

Web designers and SEO executives work hand in hand to streamline information architecture. The arrangement of pages, categories, and menus is optimized to reflect the hierarchy of information, making it easy for users to find what they are looking for. A well-organized information architecture contributes to better user engagement and search engine crawling.

3. Implementing Mobile-Responsive Design

In an era where mobile devices dominate, a mobile-responsive design is imperative for effective navigation. SEO executives consult with web designers to ensure that the website adapts seamlessly to various screen sizes and devices. This not only enhances user experience but also aligns with search engine preferences for mobile-friendly content.

Enhancing Search Engine Ranking through Design

1. Strategic Placement of Keywords

Website design becomes a canvas for SEO integration, with keywords strategically placed within elements like headers, meta tags, and image alt text. SEO executives collaborate with designers to seamlessly incorporate these elements into the design, contributing to on-page SEO and enhancing the website's relevance to search engines.

2. Optimizing Page Load Speed

Search engines prioritize websites that load quickly, and design plays a pivotal role in optimizing page load speed. SEO executives work with web designers to minimize heavy graphics, leverage browser caching, and employ compression techniques. A fast-loading website not only improves user experience but also receives preferential treatment in search engine rankings.

3. Schema Markup Implementation

SEO executives and web designers collaborate on the implementation of schema markup - a structured data format that provides additional context to search engines. By incorporating schema markup into the design, SEO practitioners enhance the visibility of rich snippets in search results, providing users with more information and improving click-through rates.

Conclusion

As we conclude this exploration into website navigation and design, it becomes evident that this realm is not a dichotomy but a seamless integration of user-centric design and strategic SEO elements. The collaborative symphony between SEO executives and web designers shapes the digital pathway, ensuring a harmonious experience for users and signaling relevance to search engines.

In the subsequent chapters of "*A Guide to SEO Executive Skills*", we will delve into analytics and reporting tools for informed decision-making, explore the intricacies of SEO performance tracking, and uncover advanced SEO strategies for digital prominence. Armed with the foundational knowledge gained here, SEO executives are poised to orchestrate the digital symphony of user experience and search engine visibility in the ever-evolving landscape of online presence.

Welcome to the realm where website navigation and design transcend the transactional and become a digital symphony - a harmonious blend of aesthetics and strategic intricacies that resonates with users and elevates a website's prominence in the competitive digital landscape.

Chapter 13. Analytics and Reporting Tools

Introduction

In the dynamic landscape of Search Engine Optimization (SEO), the ability to decipher data and glean insights is as crucial as the strategies implemented. As we navigate the chapters of *"A Guide to SEO Executive Skills"*, the exploration into analytics and reporting tools unfolds - a journey delving into the foundational experience with tools like Google Analytics, the strategic utilization of internal reporting, and the symbiotic relationship with popular keyword tools.

Analytics and reporting tools are not just instruments for number-crunching; they are the lenses through which SEO executives gain clarity on user behavior, campaign effectiveness, and overall digital performance. This chapter embarks on the exploration of how these tools form the very fabric of SEO strategy, providing actionable insights for informed decision-making.

Experience with Analytics Tools

1. Google Analytics as the Compass

At the heart of SEO analytics sits Google Analytics - a comprehensive tool that illuminates the user journey, tracks website performance, and provides invaluable insights. SEO executives harness the power of Google Analytics to understand user behavior, identify high-performing pages, and track the effectiveness of marketing campaigns. From audience demographics to page load times, Google Analytics serves as the compass guiding strategic decisions.

2. Internal Reporting for Contextual Insights

Internal reporting involves the systematic and regular communication of information within an organization, providing insights, data, and updates to aid decision-making, monitor performance, and facilitate effective communication among team members and departments. Contextual insights refer to meaningful and relevant information gained from understanding the specific circumstances, environment, or background surrounding a situation, enabling more informed decision-making or analysis.

While external analytics tools offer a panoramic view, internal reporting provides a contextualized perspective. SEO executives work with internal reporting systems to gain insights specific to their organization's goals and objectives. This may include custom dashboards, internal KPIs, and unique performance metrics tailored to the nuances of the business. KPI, or Key Performance Indicator, is a quantifiable metric used to evaluate the success or performance of an organization, department, project, or individual in achieving specific objectives or strategic goals.

3. Conversion Tracking for Goal Alignment

Google Analytics, in tandem with internal reporting, becomes a conduit for conversion tracking - an essential aspect of SEO success. SEO executives set up conversion goals aligned with business objectives, whether it's a completed purchase, a lead form submission, or another desired action. This data not only gauges campaign success but also informs strategic adjustments for enhanced performance.

Working with Popular Keyword Tools

1. Keyword Tools as Strategic Allies

In the intricate dance of SEO, keywords are the choreography that guides visibility. SEO executives leverage popular keyword tools to conduct comprehensive research, identify high-impact keywords, and understand the competitive landscape.

Ahrefs, SEMrush, and Moz are popular SEO (Search Engine Optimization) tools that provide a range of features to help website owners, marketers, and SEO professionals analyze and improve their online presence. Each tool offers capabilities such as keyword research, backlink analysis, competitor tracking, and site auditing to enhance website performance in search engine results.

2. Competitor Analysis for Strategic Advantage

Competitor analysis is the process of evaluating and studying the strengths and weaknesses of competitors in a particular market or industry. It involves gathering information on competitors' strategies, products, market share, and performance to gain insights that can inform and improve an organization's own strategic decisions and competitive positioning.

Keyword tools offer more than just keyword suggestions; they unveil the strategies employed by competitors. SEO executives conduct competitor analyses to identify gaps, discover untapped opportunities, and refine their own keyword strategies. This strategic reconnaissance contributes to staying ahead in the competitive SEO landscape.

Rank tracking, in the context of SEO (Search Engine Optimization), refers to monitoring and assessing the positions of specific keywords or webpages in search engine results over time. This process involves tracking the rankings of a website or individual pages for targeted keywords to evaluate the effectiveness of SEO efforts and identify opportunities for improvement.

SEO is not just about optimizing for keywords; it's about monitoring performance against them. Keyword tools enable rank tracking, allowing SEO executives to monitor the position of their website for target keywords over time. This continuous evaluation informs strategic adjustments to maintain or improve rankings in search engine results.

Conclusion

As we conclude this exploration into analytics and reporting tools, it becomes evident that data is not just information; it's the symphony guiding SEO executives toward mastery. The seamless integration of tools like Google Analytics, internal reporting systems, and popular keyword tools empowers practitioners to make informed decisions, refine strategies, and orchestrate the digital performance of their websites.

In the subsequent chapters of *"A Guide to SEO Executive Skills"*, we will delve into the intricacies of SEO performance tracking, explore advanced SEO strategies for digital prominence, and uncover opportunities for career growth in the ever-evolving landscape of online presence. Armed with the foundational knowledge gained here, SEO executives are poised to navigate the data tapestry and orchestrate success in the symphony of online visibility.

Welcome to the realm where analytics and reporting tools transcend the transactional and become the instruments of informed decision-making - a digital symphony that resonates with strategic clarity and SEO mastery.

Introduction

In the dynamic realm of Search Engine Optimization (SEO), success is not just about implementation; it's about continuous improvement guided by meticulous performance tracking. As we navigate the chapters of *"A Guide to SEO Executive Skills"*, the exploration into SEO performance tracking unfolds - a journey delving into strategic approaches to improve and track site performance, the art of compiling SEO performance reports, and the pivotal role these elements play in the continuous evolution of SEO strategies.

SEO performance tracking involves monitoring and analyzing various metrics and key performance indicators (KPIs) to assess the effectiveness of a website's search engine optimization efforts. This includes tracking changes in keyword rankings, organic traffic, click-through rates, conversion rates, backlink quality, and other relevant metrics to measure the impact of SEO strategies on the website's overall performance and visibility in search engine results.

SEO performance tracking is the compass that guides practitioners through the intricate landscape of digital success. It involves not just monitoring rankings but deciphering user behavior, analyzing data trends, and making strategic adjustments. This chapter embarks on the exploration of how SEO executives navigate this digital compass, strategizing ways to enhance site performance and compiling insights into comprehensive performance reports.

Strategizing Ways to Improve and Track Site Performance

1. Comprehensive Keyword Analysis

Improving site performance begins with a comprehensive keyword analysis. SEO executives delve into performance metrics associated with target keywords - monitoring rankings, analyzing click-through rates, and understanding user engagement. This data-driven approach informs adjustments to keyword strategies, ensuring alignment with user intent and search engine algorithms.

2. User Experience Optimization

Site performance is intrinsically linked to user experience. SEO executives strategize ways to optimize user experience by analyzing metrics such as bounce rates, page load times, and navigation patterns. Insights from user behavior guide adjustments to site architecture, content presentation, and overall design, enhancing the user journey and signaling relevance to search engines.

3. Backlink Profile Monitoring

The quality and relevance of backlinks significantly impact site performance. SEO executives employ tools to monitor the backlink profile, analyzing metrics such as domain authority, anchor text distribution, and the diversity of linking domains. This strategic tracking enables practitioners to identify toxic links, build authoritative backlinks, and maintain a healthy link profile.

Domain Authority (DA) is a metric developed by Moz that predicts how well a website will rank on search engine results pages. It is based on factors such as the quality and quantity of backlinks, the overall link profile, and other SEO-related elements. A higher DA suggests a stronger and more authoritative website.

Anchor text refers to the clickable text in a hyperlink. Anchor text distribution involves analyzing the variety and usage of anchor text in backlinks pointing to a website. A natural and diverse anchor text distribution is generally considered favorable for SEO, as it reflects organic and non-manipulative link-building practices.

The diversity of linking domains refers to the range of unique external websites that link to a particular domain. A diverse link profile with links from various reputable sources is considered beneficial for SEO. It indicates a more natural and authoritative online presence, as opposed to having a high number of links from a small set of domains.

These three factors are important components in assessing the overall health and authority of a website in the eyes of search engines. Site owners and SEO professionals often focus on improving these metrics as part of their strategy to enhance search engine rankings and online visibility.

Compiling and Presenting SEO Performance Reports

1. Data Visualization for Clarity

Compiling SEO performance reports involves more than presenting raw data; it requires insightful communication. SEO executives utilize data visualization tools to transform complex metrics into clear, visually compelling insights. Charts, graphs, and trends provide stakeholders with a comprehensive understanding of performance, fostering informed decision-making.

2. Aligning Reports with Business Goals

SEO performance reports are not isolated documents; they are strategic narratives aligned with business goals. SEO executives tailor reports to highlight key performance indicators (KPIs) relevant to organizational objectives. Whether it's conversion rates, revenue generated, or traffic from specific channels, reports become a means of demonstrating SEO's impact on overall business success.

3. Regular Reporting Cycles for Adaptation

The digital landscape is dynamic, and SEO performance is subject to continuous evolution. SEO executives establish regular reporting cycles - weekly, monthly, or quarterly - to track performance trends over time. Regular reporting not only enables the identification of patterns and anomalies but also facilitates adaptive strategies that align with the ever-changing digital environment.

Conclusion

As we conclude this exploration into SEO performance tracking, it becomes evident that the digital compass of success is not static; it's a dynamic symphony of continuous improvement. Strategizing ways to enhance site performance and compiling SEO performance reports are not isolated tasks but integral components of a holistic approach to SEO mastery.

In the last chapter of *"A Guide to SEO Executive Skills"*, we will delve into advanced SEO strategies, explore the intricacies of career advancement in SEO, and uncover opportunities for growth in the ever-evolving landscape of online presence. Armed with the foundational knowledge gained here, SEO executives are poised to navigate the digital compass and orchestrate success in the symphony of SEO performance.

Welcome to the realm where SEO performance tracking transcends the transactional and becomes the symphony of continuous improvement - a digital narrative that resonates with strategic clarity, adaptability, and mastery.

Chapter 15. Advanced SEO Strategies and Career Advancement

Introduction

In the culmination of "*A Guide to SEO Executive Skills*", the exploration into advanced SEO strategies and career advancement unfolds - a journey delving into the intricacies of creating sophisticated SEO strategies, staying ahead of industry trends, developing the necessary skills for role mastery, and navigating the landscape of opportunities for career growth in the ever-evolving field of SEO.

As SEO executives traverse the landscape of foundational skills and strategic insights, the pinnacle awaits - the realm of advanced SEO strategies and career elevation. This chapter marks the crescendo of the guide, inviting practitioners to embark on a journey that transcends the conventional and propels them into the echelons of digital mastery.

Creating Advanced SEO Strategies

1. Strategic Content Pruning and Expansion

Advanced SEO strategies involve a nuanced approach to content optimization. SEO executives delve into the existing content landscape, strategically pruning outdated or underperforming content while expanding and enhancing high-impact pages. This dynamic content strategy aligns with user intent, search engine algorithms, and emerging industry trends.

2. Holistic User Experience Optimization

Beyond surface-level optimizations, advanced SEO strategies encompass a holistic approach to user experience. SEO executives collaborate with web designers, developers, and content creators to orchestrate a seamless and engaging user journey. This involves optimizing not just individual pages but the entire website architecture for maximum user satisfaction.

3. Algorithmic Adaptation

Staying ahead in the digital landscape requires a keen understanding of search engine algorithms. Advanced SEO practitioners continuously monitor algorithm updates and adapt strategies accordingly. This involves anticipating algorithmic shifts, aligning content with evolving ranking factors, and implementing preemptive adjustments to maintain or enhance search engine visibility.

Search Engine Algorithms

Search engine algorithms are complex and proprietary systems developed by search engine companies (e.g., Google, Bing) to determine the ranking of web pages in search results. The exact details of these algorithms are closely guarded secrets. Search engines use algorithms to assess various factors and deliver the most relevant and high-quality results to users. Here are general guidelines on how to optimize for search engine algorithms:

1. Quality Content

> Create high-quality, relevant, and valuable content that meets the needs of users.

- ➢ Use clear and engaging language, and provide information that is authoritative and trustworthy.

2. Keyword Optimization

- ➢ Conduct keyword research to understand the terms users are searching for.
- ➢ Naturally incorporate relevant keywords into your content, titles, and meta tags.

3. User Experience

- ➢ Design your website for a positive user experience with easy navigation and a mobile-friendly layout.
- ➢ Ensure fast page load times to improve user satisfaction.

4. Backlinks

- ➢ Build a diverse and natural backlink profile with links from authoritative and relevant sources.
- ➢ Focus on earning quality backlinks rather than engaging in manipulative practices.

5. Technical SEO

- ➢ Optimize technical aspects of your website, including crawlability, sitemaps, and URL structure.
- ➢ Use descriptive and SEO-friendly URLs.

6. Social Signals

- ➢ Engage with users on social media platforms and encourage social sharing of your content.
- ➢ While social signals are not direct ranking factors, they can contribute to increased visibility.

7. Secure and Accessible Website

> - Ensure your website is secure with HTTPS.
> - Make sure search engines can easily crawl and index your site by using a robots.txt file and submitting a sitemap.

8. Regular Updates

> - Keep your content up-to-date and relevant.
> - Regularly update and improve your website to stay current with industry trends and user expectations.

It's important to note that search engine algorithms are dynamic and frequently updated. Keeping abreast of algorithm changes and industry best practices is crucial for maintaining and improving search rankings. While understanding general SEO principles is valuable, gaining access to the specific algorithms of major search engines is not possible, as they are closely guarded intellectual property. SEO professionals rely on observations, industry knowledge, and testing to adapt their strategies to algorithm updates.

Staying Ahead of Industry Trends

1. Continuous Learning and Professional Development

The digital landscape is a dynamic canvas, and staying ahead requires a commitment to continuous learning. Advanced SEO executives invest in professional development, attending industry conferences, participating in webinars, and enrolling in courses to stay abreast of emerging trends, tools, and best practices.

2. Trend Analysis and Forecasting

Beyond reacting to trends, advanced SEO practitioners engage in proactive trend analysis and forecasting. By analyzing industry trends, consumer behavior, and technological advancements, they position themselves as thought leaders capable of not just adapting to change but influencing the trajectory of SEO strategies.

3. Innovation in Emerging Technologies

The digital ecosystem is not static; it evolves with technological advancements. Advanced SEO executives embrace emerging technologies such as artificial intelligence, voice search, and mobile innovations. By integrating these technologies into their strategies, they position themselves at the forefront of digital innovation.

Developing Necessary Skills for the Role

1. Advanced Data Analysis and Interpretation

Beyond basic analytics, advanced SEO practitioners possess advanced data analysis skills. They leverage tools for in-depth data interpretation, uncovering nuanced insights that inform strategic decisions. This skill involves proficiency in data visualization, statistical analysis, and the ability to extract actionable recommendations from complex datasets.

2. Programming Proficiency for Technical SEO

As SEO evolves, technical skills become a differentiator. Advanced SEO executives develop programming proficiency, enabling them to navigate the technical intricacies of websites, implement structured data, and troubleshoot technical issues. This skill set positions them as comprehensive SEO strategists capable of optimizing every facet of a digital presence.

3. Strategic Leadership and Communication

Advancement in SEO often involves leadership roles where effective communication and strategic thinking are paramount. Advanced SEO practitioners hone their leadership and communication skills, ensuring they can articulate complex strategies to diverse stakeholders, lead cross-functional teams, and drive organizational alignment with SEO objectives.

Exploring Opportunities for Career Growth in SEO

1. Leadership Roles in SEO Management

With advanced skills and a strategic mindset, career growth often leads to leadership roles in SEO management. Advanced SEO executives transition into positions where they orchestrate holistic SEO strategies, guide teams, and contribute to organizational growth through enhanced online visibility.

2. Entrepreneurial Ventures and Consulting

Some advanced SEO practitioners explore entrepreneurial ventures, establishing their agencies or consultancy firms. This pathway allows them to leverage their expertise for diverse clients, shape industry practices, and contribute to the broader ecosystem through thought leadership.

3. Educational Roles and Thought Leadership

As digital experts, advanced SEO executives find opportunities to contribute to the education and thought leadership within the industry. This may involve roles in academia, where they share their knowledge with the next generation of digital marketers, or thought leadership through writing articles, speaking at conferences, and participating in industry forums.

4. Specialized Verticals and Industries

Career growth in SEO often opens doors to specialized verticals and industries. Advanced practitioners may choose to focus on specific sectors such as healthcare, finance, or e-commerce, where their in-depth knowledge of SEO can be applied to address unique challenges and opportunities within those domains.

Conclusion

As we conclude this exploration into advanced SEO strategies and career advancement, it becomes evident that the summit of SEO excellence is not a destination but a continual journey of growth and adaptation. The landscape of SEO is ever-evolving, and advanced practitioners are the navigators shaping its course.

In the journey through "*A Guide to SEO Executive Skills*", we have traversed the foundational principles, honed strategic insights, and reached the zenith of digital mastery. Armed with advanced SEO strategies, a commitment to staying ahead of industry trends, and a toolbox of expertise, SEO executives are poised for not just success but leadership in the dynamic world of online visibility.

The symphony of SEO excellence continues, and the practitioners who embrace innovation, continuous learning, and strategic leadership will find themselves not just navigating the digital landscape but shaping its contours. As the SEO journey unfolds, the possibilities for growth, impact, and contribution to the digital ecosystem are boundless.

Welcome to the summit of SEO excellence - a realm where advanced strategies meet career elevation, and practitioners become architects of digital success. The journey doesn't end here; it transforms into an ever-evolving exploration of what's possible in the dynamic and fascinating world of SEO.

"A Guide to SEO Executive Skills" is an essential companion for navigating the dynamic world of search engine optimization. This comprehensive guide explores the fundamentals of SEO, from understanding search engines to practical strategies like website analysis, keyword research, and on-page optimization. It delves into technical skills, ethical practices, and advanced SEO strategies, offering insights for both beginners and seasoned professionals.

Whether you're optimizing content or tracking performance, this book provides a roadmap for success in the evolving field of SEO, making it an indispensable resource for those aspiring to excel in their roles and explore career growth opportunities.

ABOUT THE AUTHOR

Mr. C. P. Kumar is a retired Scientist 'G' from National Institute of Hydrology, Roorkee, Uttarakhand, India. He is also a Reiki Healer and Chakra Balancing practitioner (with pendulum dowsing) and offers Emotional Freedom Technique (EFT) to help individuals with emotional issues. Mr. Kumar has authored many books on technical, spiritual, and social topics.

For further details, you may visit his webpage
https://www.angelfire.com/nh/cpkumar/virgo.html